First published in Great Britain 2022 by Red Shed, part of Farshore
An imprint of HarperCollins*Publishers*
1 London Bridge Street, London SE1 9GF
www.farshore.co.uk

HarperCollins*Publishers*
1st Floor, Watermarque Building, Ringsend Road
Dublin 4, Ireland

Text copyright © HarperCollins*Publishers* Limited 2022
Written by Susie Brooks.
Illustrations copyright © Josy Bloggs 2022
Josy Bloggs has asserted her moral rights.

ISBN 978 1 4052 9908 4
Printed in UK by Pureprint a CarbonNeutral® Company.
001

Consultancy by Dr Fiona Russell.

A CIP catalogue record for this title is available from the British Library.

Stay safe online. Any website addresses listed in this book are correct at the time of going to print.
However, Farshore is not responsible for content hosted by third parties. Please be aware that online
content can be subject to change and websites can contain content that is unsuitable for children.
We advise that all children are supervised when using the internet.

For my amazing mum and dad,
whose recipes made me! – S.B.

To Yasmin, my family and
other animals – J.B.

YOU ARE 25% BANANA

Written by Susie Brooks
Illustrated by Josy Bloggs

RED SHED

Are you a banana?

Not unless you have yellow peel and taste good with custard!

But a banana is more like you than you might think, if you open up its RECIPE BOOK . . .

All living things, including fruits and people, have built-in 'recipes' called GENES.

And about a quarter of the recipes needed to make a human are the SAME as ones you'll find in a BANANA.

That's right, about **25%** of your genes match genes in this squishy fruit.

Genes are the recipes that make you YOU!

They decide what colour your hair is,
how long your legs (and neck!) are . . .
and if you have legs at all or just a stalk.

Genes do lots and lots of jobs,
telling every part of your body
how to work and grow.

You get half of them from
your dad and half
from your mum.

That means you're a **magic mix**
of both your parents.

Some gene recipes are
BOSSIER
than others.

That's why some hair or eye colours
are more common.

For instance, more humans have brown
eyes than blue. And most tigers are
ORANGE with AMBER eyes . . .

. . . but a few tigers are
WHITE with BLUE eyes!

You have **thousands** of genes . . . but **rice** has even more!

There are about **25,000** genes in your recipe book.

A teeny grain of rice has about **36,000.**

A bald eagle has around **15,000** genes.

A sunflower has roughly **52,000** genes.

An apple has over **56,000** genes.

Great white sharks have about **25,000** genes.

Pandas have about **21,000.**

An octopus has around **30,000.**

Even bamboo has about **32,000** genes.

But having **more genes** in your recipe book isn't always more useful. Sometimes the same recipe is just repeated over and over again.

You share
SINGING
genes with birds.

Humans, songbirds and parrots all have genes that help us learn new sounds and tunes.

You share **TOOTH-GROWING** genes with sharks.

In fact, your teeth are as strong as a shark's! But while you only grow two sets of teeth, sharks can grow many more.

You share **BRAINY** genes with dolphins.

Dolphins can solve puzzles, learn tricks and recognize themselves in a mirror, just like you can.

You're related to daffodils, dogs . . . even **dung beetles!**

Every living thing on Earth came from the same family originally.
We know this because all our recipes are written using a code
of the same four letters: A, C, G and T.

ATCAGGACT
ACGATTAGC
TCAGGACTA
TAGGCTCAG
GACCTGTTT
GGGCGTTAC

TAGTCCTGA
TGCTAATCG
AGTCCTGAT
ATCCGAGGG
CTGGACAAA
CCCGCAATG

So we're all related, but are you more similar
to a chicken or a mouse? Let's take a look
and see how closely other animals'
genes match yours . . .

Fruit flies are 60% like you!

Yes, 60 out of every 100 recipes
in their recipe book are
similar to yours.

Fruit flies share so many of
our genes, they have even
been sent on space missions.

Studying them can help us learn how space travel affects the human body.

Chickens are
60%
like you!

The muscles in your arms are very like the ones that help chickens flap their wings.

Chickens are one of the closest living relatives of dinosaurs. Luckily their recipe book doesn't give them teeth like T. rex!

Genes are far too tiny to see, but they come in twisty ladder shapes, a bit like this.

Mice are 75% like you!

Humans and mice share tail-growing genes – but our tail genes 'switch off' before we're born.

Cows are 80% like you!

They feed their babies milk, just like humans do.

Cats are 90% like you!

Perhaps that's why we both like
climbing trees?

Pet cats also share most of their genes with lions.
But while cats can purr, they can't roar.
Lions *can* roar, but they can't purr!

Chimps are 99% like you!

They make friends and laugh and play, much the same as we do.
But chimps DON'T TALK and they mostly walk on FOUR LEGS!
So are we really that alike?

Well . . . nearly 99 out of every 100 recipes in your recipe book match theirs. But each different recipe contains thousands of instructions that make you less of a chimp!

You're **99.9%** identical to every other person in the whole world.

Nearly all of your genes are just like everyone else's.
Just ONE in every THOUSAND recipes in your
recipe book is different enough to make you . . .
YOU!